CASPIAN SEA

Cyrus

Araxes

Lake Van

Lake Urmia

MEDIA

ELBURZ MOUNTAINS

SSYRIA

•Nineveh

Ashur •

Tigris

MESOPOTAMIA

ZAGROS MOUNTAINS

The hanging gardens of Babylon

Babylon•

Kish

Susa•

BABYLONIA

ELAM

DESERT

Erech•
Ur ɪ

The Ziggurat at Ur (a famous temple-tower)

ARABIAN GULF

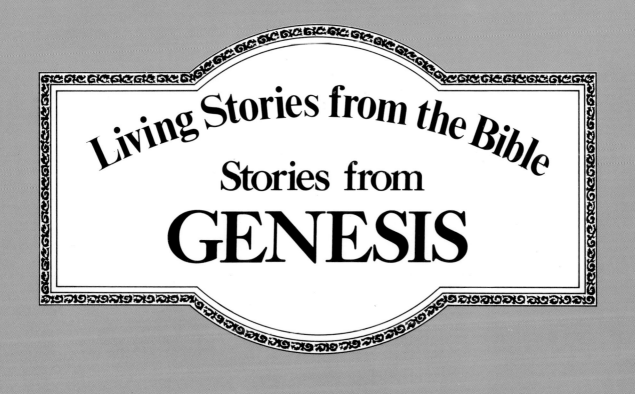

Living Stories from the Bible
Stories from
GENESIS

Hutchinson
London Melbourne Sydney Auckland Johannesburg

Foreword

THERE IS A SENSE IN WHICH THE BIBLE has to be rewritten for every generation. Otherwise it becomes a relic of the past, an ancient book encased in black covers and exclusively associated with the Church. But the Bible is for all mankind, young and old, black and white, 20th century or 1st century. This new publication fulfils the purpose which animated those who produced it, i.e. to make the Bible live for the young (and the young in heart) in the way in which it has lived in the hearts and minds of men for 2000 years and more. The stories are vividly (and accurately) told; the illustrations are magnificent and the literary format easy to follow. I congratulate the authors, the illustrators and the publishers on a singularly attractive publication.

Stuart Ebor: (Archbishop of York)

THE BIBLE HAS TO BE SEEN, not so much as history to be studied, as an invitation to God's way of life for us. Various literary forms are used and it is important that from an early age we are enabled to understand their meaning. In presentation to children, the Old Testament books are perhaps inevitably taken more or less literally. But here a fair balance has been preserved and the adaptation of the New Testament material shows considerable skill and sensitivity. With the exciting illustrations, the whole should do much to develop among young readers an interest in the Bible which should lead to a developing love and appreciation for the history of man's salvation.

†Derek Worlock (Roman Catholic Archbishop of Liverpool)

AUTHORS
Meryl and Malcolm Doney

EDITOR
John Grisewood

ARTISTS
Harry Bishop   Tudor Art

OLD TESTAMENT CONSULTANT
Alan Millard
Rankin Senior Lecturer in Hebrew
and Ancient Semitic Languages,
Liverpool University

ADVISORY PANEL
Reverend John Huxtable DD
Reverend Gilbert Kirby
Sister Mary Richardson

Published by Hutchinson Junior Books Ltd
3 Fitzroy Square London W1
An imprint of the Hutchinson Publishing Group

First published 1981

Designed and produced by Grisewood & Dempsey Ltd
Grosvenor House, 141/143 Drury Lane, London WC2

ISBN 0 09 144320 2

Printed and bound by Leefung-Asco Printers Ltd., Hong Kong

Contents

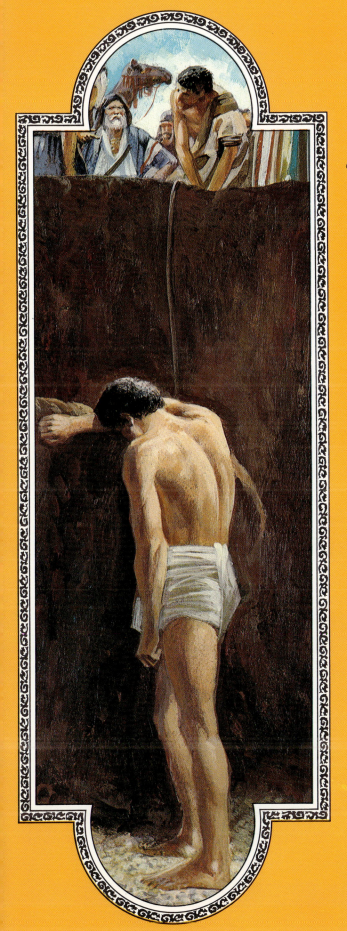

History with a purpose

THE BIBLE'S FIRST WORDS ARE: "In the beginning God created the universe...". Immediately we are back at the very start of our world—the dawn of time.

In a poetic and moving way God's creation of the universe unfolds—the sea, land, plants and animals, made from nothing, new and free. Then comes God's ultimate creation, mankind. It is not an historical or scientific account. Its purpose is to say that everything was created by God.

After the Creation story, the Bible relates a series of fascinating and often exciting stories about God's dealings with men and women. Adam and Eve—mankind—disobey God and turn their backs on freedom. Evil enters the paradise world God has created. The first murder is committed. One family escapes from a catastrophic flood in a floating zoo, crammed with animals of every description. A group of people are so carried away by their early discoveries that they believe themselves to be gods! So begins an account of man on this earth.

The Bible then records a seemingly insignificant event that marks the origin of one of the most important and remarkable families in history. A young man named Abram sets out from the city of Ur in Mesopotamia. As his story unfolds, his unshakeable faith in God leads to his being called "the friend of God" and to the promise that he will be the father of a great nation.

The saga of his family, with its faith and courage, yet its plots and intrigues, jealousy and violence, makes exciting reading, as it is slowly transformed into God's own people—Israel.

But this is not simply a chronicle of important events as the nation of Israel begins to take shape. It is a history written with a special purpose—a record of God's relationship with the world. Ultimately, it is about the working of God's will in the lives of men and women so that mankind, his creation, shall be saved.

In the beginning God created the heavens and earth. The earth was without form and void, and darkness was upon the face of the deep; and the Spirit of God was moving over the face of the waters.
And God said, "Let there be light"; and there was light.
Genesis 1:1–3

The Story of the Creation

IN FAR DISTANT DAYS THE HEBREW PEOPLE of the Bible were a wandering tribe earning a meagre living by moving from place to place with their flocks and herds in search of new grazing land. In the evening, when they had pitched their tents, they would sit under the vast vault of the star-studded sky and chat and relate familiar stories that had been passed on by word of mouth from father to son. Some of these stories gave answers to age-old questions—"Who made this wonderful world?" "Who created the animals?" "Who is man?" "Why do people quarrel and fight?" In all these stories the Spirit of God guided the early Hebrew people to the answers and to the truths by which to know him.

One of the stories tells how the world began. It is not a first-hand historical account, because no one was there. There are no technical or scientific details, no dates or times. It is a true account nonetheless, for God's Spirit had enabled his people to understand his world and how it came into being. It tells us that the Universe has a Creator who made it beautiful, rich and free. He has a purpose in his work and his plans are still being worked out. There is an all-powerful yet loving Creator who knows each one of us personally.

This is how the story has come down to us.

In the beginning, when God created the universe, the earth was empty and uninhabitable. The

heaving ocean that covered everything was wrapped in total darkness. God's Spirit moved like a bird over the waters.

Then God spoke and his Word created.

"Let there be light," he commanded, and the world was bathed in brilliance. God was pleased with what he saw. He separated the light from the darkness. The light became day and the darkness became night. *Evening and morning had come—the first day.*

At God's command the sky, earth's atmosphere, was made. It spread like a huge dome above the empty earth, giving the world air to breathe. *Evening passed and morning came—a second day.*

At God's command dry land rose up from the great waters. The land he called earth and the water, sea. At God's command life came to the earth. A sheen of rich green spread over the surface. Then grasses sprang up and plants of all kinds. Their roots went deep into the soil and they produced flowers and fruit. God was pleased with what he saw. *Evening passed and morning came—a third day.*

God set the earth among the brilliant stars. He caused the sun to shine on the earth, making the day. The cool, clear moon lit the night. The movements of sun, moon and stars measured days and seasons for the earth. *Evening passed and morning came—a fourth day.*

Now God commanded, "Let the waters be filled with life and let birds fly in the sky." The seas teemed with all kinds of creatures and the sky was filled with birds wheeling and diving in flight. God was pleased with what he saw. He blessed his creatures and commanded them to increase in number until they filled the earth. *Evening passed and morning came—a fifth day.*

Then God commanded, "Let the earth produce all kinds of animal life, domestic and wild, large and small." So animals began to roam over the earth—from huge beasts to tiny insects. God was pleased with what he saw. It was good.

Now the world was ready for God's final great act of creation. "They will be like me and they will be able to know me," he said. "They will have power over the fish, the birds and all the animals."

Out of the newly formed earth, God made Man. He breathed life into him so that he would be like his creator. God called the Man Adam.

Then God said, "It is not good that man should be alone. I will make a companion for him." Taking a bone out of his side, God created a woman. He called her Eve, meaning Life. Then, blessing the two people who had been made for each other, he said: "Have many children so that your descendants fill the earth. You are the masters over my world—all the fish, birds and animals. I have given you grain and fruit to eat and grasses and leaves for the animals." *Evening passed and morning came—a sixth day.*

On the seventh day the Lord God rested. By resting he made a special pattern for all his creatures. They could work for six days but the next was to be a day of rest. He blessed the seventh day and it was called holy, a day set apart for God. *Evening passed and morning came—a seventh day.*
Genesis 1 and 2:1-3

The Message of the Creation story
The story of the creation tells us some important things about the world we live in:
● There is a creator: God.
    The existence of the universe is no accident.
● God made everything in the universe.
● All that God made was good.
● The most important single thing that God created was Man himself.
● People differ from the rest of creation in two important ways: they are made in the image of God; and they have been given the responsibility of looking after God's world.

Then God said, "Let us make man in our image, after our likeness; and let them have dominion over the fish of the sea, and over the birds of the air, and over the cattle, and over all the earth . . ." So God created man in his own image, in the image of God he created him; male and female he created them.
Genesis 1:26-27

Adam and Eve in the Garden

"HOW DID EVIL ENTER THE WORLD?" is a question that has been asked for countless centuries. The early people of Bible times answered this question by telling this tragic story.

The story is set in a beautiful garden that God made for Adam and Eve to live in. God called it Eden.

In the centre of this garden stood the magnificent Tree of Life. There also, God planted a special tree. It held the secret of the knowledge of good and evil.

"This is your garden," God told the man Adam and his wife Eve. "It is rich with everything you need. You can eat your fill of fruit from the trees. But you must not eat of the Tree of the Knowledge of Good and Evil. If you eat the fruit from that tree you will die."

Apart from this one thing, Adam and Eve were free to do whatever they wanted. There were the animals to name and look after and the whole world to explore and cultivate. They could walk with God himself, in the cool of the evening, in friendship and trust. All their days were busy and happy.

Mysteriously sin entered the world. Even in this beautiful garden there was a dark presence. Satan, the evil one, looked at the perfect world and hated it. He would spoil it if he could. It might be possible to turn Adam and Eve against God.

The story goes that the evil one took the shape of a snake and coiled itself in the branches of God's special tree. "Eve," he called, so softly that it was like a voice in her head. "Did God really tell you not to eat any of these delicious fruits?" "We can eat fruit from any of the trees in the garden," she said, "except for this one. God said that if we even touch it, we will die."

"You won't die," hissed the snake. "If you eat the fruit you will be like God. You will know what he knows. That is what it means to have the knowledge of good and evil."

Eve began to feel less sure of herself. What if the snake were right? Wouldn't it be wonderful to know everything? Slowly, she stretched out her hand, picked one of the beautiful fruits and ate it. With no further thought of what she had done, she offered the fruit to Adam. He, too, knew that he should have refused, but he did not. He ate some of the fruit.

Suddenly, they both felt guilty and ashamed. Their eyes were opened to see that life was no longer simple and innocent. God had trusted them and they had betrayed him. They were ashamed of being naked and tried to cover themselves with leaves.

With the guilt and shame came fear. Suppose God found out?

That evening they heard God walking in the garden as usual. They hid in the trees, hoping he might go away. God called out to Adam, "Where are you?" "I heard you," replied Adam, "but I was afraid, so I hid."

It was then that the whole tragic story of the disobedience came out.

"Eve gave me the fruit and I ate it," Adam told God.

The Lord God turned to Eve, "Why?" he asked. "The snake tempted me," she said.

There was a faint rustling among the leaves. God turned on the snake. "You will be punished for this," he said. "You will crawl in the dust and this woman and her children will be your sworn enemies. You will bite them and they will crush you underfoot."

To Eve he said: "Because of what you have done, giving birth will be painful. But you must love your husband who shall be your master."

To Adam God said: "Adam, you listened to your wife rather than to me and have disobeyed me. Because of what you have done, the earth which helped you to produce food, will now be your enemy. You will sweat to grow your daily bread. And one day you will both die. Dust you are and unto dust you will return."

God then turned Adam and Eve out of their garden home. It had been spoiled by their disobedience. God could no longer trust them.

He set the Cherubim, the angelic guards, to bar the way back with flaming swords. Man would not see the Tree of Life again.

So man and woman began to live in toil and to have children and people the earth.

Genesis 2 and 3

. . . and at the east of the garden of Eden God placed the Cherubim, and a flaming sword which turned every way, to guard the way to the tree of life.

Genesis 3:24

The Story of Cain and Abel

... Cain brought to the Lord an offering of the fruit of the ground, and Abel brought of the firstlings of his flock and of their fat portions. And the Lord had regard for Abel and his offering, but for Cain and his offering he had no regard. So Cain was very angry and his countenance fell.
Genesis 4: 3–4

THROUGH DISOBEDIENCE TO GOD evil had entered the world and so the man Adam and his wife Eve had been driven out of the Garden of Eden. In time two sons were born to them. The elder son was called Cain, the younger was called Abel. Their story is a terrible example of what jealousy and anger can lead to.

As they grew up Cain became a farmer and Abel became a shepherd.

They knew that they owed their life to God and so it was natural that at harvest time they should give thanks to him for good crops and healthy animals. They did this by holding a simple festival and offering on an altar some of what they had grown or reared during the year.

Abel, the shepherd, brought the first-born lamb of his flocks. He killed it and offered the best parts of the animal to the Lord. He did so willingly and out of a genuinely thankful heart. God was pleased by what he had done.

Cain brought some of his crops to offer to God, but it seemed to Cain that God took no notice of his gift. Cain may not have been truly grateful to God for his help; he may have made the offering unwillingly; or perhaps he was too proud of his own efforts. But God was not pleased with Cain's offering. And Cain knew it. Cain became angry and sullen. His face was black with bitter rage at his rejection and he was insanely jealous of his younger brother.

God said to Cain, "Why are you so angry? You know well that if you had offered me these gifts in love you could hold your head up high now. But you have done wrong. Do not let it take you over. Evil is real and is waiting like a hungry beast to get hold of you. You must overcome it."

But Cain paid no attention. He was filled with jealousy. Soon he met Abel. "Abel," he said apparently innocently, "Let us walk in the fields." Suspecting nothing, Abel agreed and they wandered off together.

Suddenly Cain picked up a rock, rounded on Abel and smashed it into his skull. Abel fell to the ground lifeless.

Cain ran blindly through the fields, but he could not get away. God's voice came to him clear and searching. "Where is your brother, Cain?" Cain tried to pretend that nothing had happened. Then he made matters worse. He lied to God. "I don't know where Abel is," he said. "How am I supposed to know? Am I my brother's keeper?"

"Cain, why have you done this terrible thing?" asked God. "I can almost hear your brother's blood, like a voice crying out for vengeance. You will be punished for what you have done. It will be as if Abel's blood has poisoned the earth for you. You were a good farmer; now you will not be able to grow anything. You will spend your life as a homeless wanderer."

Cain cried out, "This punishment is too hard for me to bear. You are driving me off the land

and away from your presence. Anyone who finds me will kill me."

"No," said God. "Murder is still murder. If anyone kills you, revenge will be taken."

So Cain was shut from the presence of God and lived as a nomad in the lands to the East of Eden where he became the head of a new tribe.
Genesis 4: 1-16

Then the Lord said to Cain, "Where is Abel your brother?" He said, "I do not know; am I my brother's keeper?"
Genesis 4:9

Noah and the Great Flood

EN NEEDED TO BE WARNED that they will do evil when they break away from God, and disaster will follow. So they told this story of Noah. It tells of a time long, long ago when the sons and daughters of Man had become cruel and thoughtless and violent. They killed and stole, lied and cheated and thought of nothing but wickedness. God looked down on the world which he had made. He was deeply hurt. He felt sorry that he had ever created the human race. "I will rid earth's face of man," he said.

But there was one person who truly worshipped God. His name was Noah. He was an honest and straightforward man who tried to live his life as God wanted. Because of this, God decided to spare Noah and his family from the punishment he must bring on the world of men.

God spoke to Noah. "I have decided to put a stop to the evil in the world." He told Noah he would send a great flood that would wipe out all his people—except for Noah and his family.

"Noah," said God, "build a boat for yourself out of good timber. It should have three decks, divided into rooms, and a door at the side. Make it watertight with pitch."

God gave Noah the exact measurements for the boat, or ark as it was called. It would be like an enormous floating container. But why, wondered Noah, was there so much space just for himself, his wife, his three sons and their wives?

"Collect males and females of every kind of animal and bird there is," God went on, "and take them into the boat with you. Then, when the flood is over they will be able to re-populate the earth with animal life." God also reminded Noah to take on board huge supplies of food.

Noah obeyed God. He and his sons, Ham, Shem, and Japheth, set to work. How the people stared and laughed as they saw them building the great boat on dry land, miles away from the nearest sea. But Noah kept on building. He cut the wood, dragged it into place, pegged the great beams together, and painted on the last of the pitch.

At last the magnificent boat was finished. God told Noah to collect the animals. In they went, two by two—elephants, lions, deer, rabbits, foxes, lizards, monkeys, eagles, everything. Then Noah and his family went into the boat.

Soon, just as God had warned, dark clouds began to gather overhead, until the sky was black. Suddenly the sky seemed to break and torrential rain poured down like a waterfall. At the same time, underground streams burst to the surface and flooded the land.

Slowly the water rose, drowning trees and fields, flooding the cities, and rising until it covered the hilltops. Every living thing perished.

After 40 terrible days there was a calm outside the boat. The storms seemed spent and no more rain fell. The water began to go down. But it was to be several months before the mountain peaks began to break through the surface of the grey water.

More time passed. Noah now decided to send out a raven to see if it could find dry land. It did not come back. Later he sent out a dove but it could not find the dry, sheltered place it needed

---

The Flood—did it really happen?
There is archaeological evidence to suggest that a great flood that destroyed "all the works of man" really took place—at least on that part of the earth known to the people who lived in Mesopotamia. It was from a city called Ur in Mesopotamia that Abraham originally came.

In 1929 Sir Leonard Woolley was excavating the royal cemetery at Ur. He dated finds there to about 2800 BC. But he wanted to learn more about the ancestry of these people, so he decided to dig deeper to lower levels of the remains. After he had dug through about one metre there were no more 'finds', only water laid mud. He dug through several more metres when suddenly flints and pottery appeared again. He dug in another part of the site, with the same result. The evidence pointed to the clear soil having been deposited by a widespread flood.

and returned to the boat. After seven days Noah tried again. Off flew the dove over the waters. That evening it returned. In its beak it carried a fresh green olive leaf. "The waters are going down and the trees are appearing again," Noah cried joyfully. A week later he set the dove free again. This time it did not come back.

The water had gone and the ark came to rest on a peak of Mount Ararat. Noah took the covering off the top of the ark. Light and air streamed in. Noah and his family finally stepped out on dry land followed by all the creatures, great and small, from the massive elephant to the tiny shrew. They left the boat as·they had entered it—two by two. The world was empty, waiting for a new start.

Then Noah built an altar to God and in thanksgiving offered sacrifices of birds and animals. God was pleased with Noah's thanks and made a solemn promise. "Never again will I flood the world to destroy all the people I have made. As long as the world exists, there will be a time for planting and a time for harvesting, cold and heat, summer and winter, day and night." Then God said, "Look up and see the rainbow in the sky when the sun shines upon rain. That is the sign of my pact." Noah looked up and there, stretched across the sky, was a beautiful rainbow.
Genesis 6 : 5-22 ; 7, 8, and 9 :1-17

Then God said to Noah, "Go forth from the ark, you and your wife, and your sons and your sons' wives with you. Bring forth with you every living thing that is with you of all flesh – birds, and animals and every creeping thing that creeps on the earth – that they may breed abundantly on the earth, and be fruitful and multiply upon the earth."
Genesis 8 : 15–17

The Tower of Babel

AFTER THE GREAT FLOOD the centuries passed and the population of the world increased. Everyone in the world, it was believed, spoke the same language and understood one another.

At some time during those centuries a great migration of people took place. They settled in the Babylonian plain. There, a great civilization grew up. Things were going well for them. There was plenty to eat and everyone lived comfortable lives. But the people began to forget God, they became arrogant and proud.

"With our new discovery," said one man, rising to his feet, "we'll build the biggest city the world has ever known. In the centre we can build a tower that will reach right up in the sky! It will stand so high that everyone will be able to see it for miles around. Then they will know what we are capable of!" There was a chorus of agreement among the Babylonian people.

The great discovery they had made was how to make bricks. They could bake them so hard that they were able to make huge buildings that would last for years. Now they were talking about building a fantastic tower to show off their skill. Not once did they think to thank God for giving them the skill or the raw materials or the prosperity that made the whole thing possible.

The planning continued. "We'll use the new bricks, hold them together with tar and make the tower so that it reaches right up to the sky," said one "Yes, a tower like that will act as a landmark and keep us all together."

If they had really thought about it, they would have had to admit they meant to show that they were totally independent of God. They had begun to believe that they were so powerful and clever they could do anything. It was a short step to declare that they were God themselves.

God was angry. This was just the beginning of a major rebellion. Violence and lawlessness would follow, everyone doing just what they wanted, and soon the world would be as bad as it had been before the flood.

Work on the great tower, the centre-piece of the city, began. Slowly it climbed higher and higher. They were still building the upper levels of the great monument to man's achievement when God said, "Enough!"

Then suddenly, throughout the great city something amazing happened. People were not speaking the same language any more. One man would try to say something to his neighbour only to be met with blank astonishment. When the man replied, it sounded like babble. God had divided their language. People could no longer communicate with one another. No one could understand what the foreman wanted and the foreman could not understand what his workers were saying. The building of the tower had to be abandoned.

Slowly groups formed who discovered they had the same language. People kept with those they could talk to. They no longer all worked together. Overnight the idea of building a city where they could all live, seemed ridiculous.

At a stroke God had shown that, clever as the people of Babel were, there was only one God, only one Lord of all the Universe. The story was really trying to give an explanation of how the different languages of the world began: from Babel groups of people speaking the same language drifted away from one another and settled in new regions as new nations.

Genesis 11 : 1-9

God's Promise to Abram

WITH THE STORY OF ABRAHAM and those that follow we begin the history of God's Chosen People, Israel, of whom Abraham—at first called Abram— was the founding father. The stories were told by people who lived then. They were handed down by word of mouth and sometimes written down in chronicles.

In Mesopotamia, in the splendid city of Ur with its fine buildings and temples to many gods, there lived a wealthy man called Terah who had three sons. One son, Abram, was married to a beautiful woman named Sarai, but she had no children. Late in his life Terah left Ur taking with him his family, their servants, flocks and possessions and travelled northwards to a place called Haran.

When Terah died, Abram had a strange experience. It seemed to him that there was only one God of all creation who should be worshipped and that that God was speaking to him. "Leave here and go to a land I will show you. I am going to give you many descendants and they will become a great nation. You will do well in that land and your name will become famous. Through you I am going to bless all nations."

Such instructions and promises could not be ignored. So Abram set off south-westwards to Canaan, the land God had set aside for him. He took his wife and nephew Lot, together with his

And Abram took Sarai his wife,
and Lot his brother's son, and all
their possessions which they had
gathered, and the persons that they
had gotten in Haran; and they set
forth to go to the land of Canaan.
Genesis 12:5

fighting men, workers, slaves and large herds of sheep and cattle. When he arrived in the region, he built an altar and there God appeared to him again. "This is the country I am going to give your family," he said to Abram.

But the time was not right for settling. Other tribes owned the land and Canaan had been hit by a serious famine. So Abram moved farther south to Egypt. Here they could live until it was time to return. But one thing worried Abram. Sarai his wife was beautiful and he was sure that the Egyptians would want to make her one of the wives of the pharaoh. They would probably kill him to do so. "Sarai," he said to his wife. "Tell the Egyptian authorities that you are my sister, then we'll all be safe."

Abram's fears were justified. As soon as they crossed the border Sarai was taken to the palace to become part of the pharaoh's household. But his plan worked. Abram was not harmed. In order to gain favour with him to win his 'sister' for the pharaoh, he was treated as an important person. He was given slaves, sheep, goats, cattle and camels.

Even though the pharaoh had taken Sarai to his court in ignorance, God was not going to let him endanger his plan for Abram's descendants. A series of terrible diseases broke out in the palace and the pharaoh saw the judgement of God in them. He sent for Abram. "Why didn't you tell me she was your wife?" he demanded. "There, take her back and get out!" He gave orders to his soldiers to send Abram, Sarai and all his belongings out of the country.

The company travelled back north again towards Canaan, and headed for Bethel where Abram's altar had been set up. There they worshipped God again. But all was not well with the community. Abram was a rich man with a large household and large herds of sheep, cattle, and goats. Lot, too, had many possessions. There was seldom enough pasture for all the animals. Before long serious quarrels broke out between Abram's herdsmen and those of Lot.

Abram wisely suggested that they should separate to save argument. "We are kinsmen," he said to Lot. "We should not quarrel. Choose any part of the land you want. You go your way and I'll go mine." Lot had enjoyed the good life in Egypt and chose the rich Jordan Valley with its well-watered pastures and thriving cities. He settled on the outskirts of the city of Sodom.

Abram moved up into the hill-country of Hebron. There, he built an altar to the Lord and worshipped him.

Sometime later, news reached Abram that a tribal war had broken out. Four local chiefs had formed an alliance against five others. Fighting raged over a wide area of the countryside. Sodom had fallen, Lot had been captured and all his possessions taken away. One of his men managed to escape and to reach Abram with the news.

Immediately Abram called his 318 fighting men together, and set off in pursuit of the captors. When they caught up with them, Abram launched a commando raid at night. It was successful and Abram was able to rescue Lot as well as the other prisoners and to take back all the loot.

On his return, two kings came to see Abram. The first was the King of Sodom who had been defeated. He said to Abram "You can keep the gold but give me back my people." But Abram would not keep a single thing. He did not want to be in debt to the King of Sodom in any way.

The second visitor was Melchizedek, King of Salem, the city later ages called Jerusalem. He was also a priest, worshipping the true God, just as Abram did.

Melchizedek brought him gifts of bread and wine and pronounced a solemn blessing on Abram. "May the Most High God, who made heaven and earth, bless Abram," he said. Abram, realizing that this man came from God himself, gave him a tenth of all the riches he had captured, as an offering.

There was no doubt about it. God was protecting Abram, preparing him to be the father of a great nation. Shortly after the visit of Melchizedek, Abram had a vision. He heard God saying to him, "Do not be afraid Abram. I will shield you from danger and give you a great reward." When he heard this, Abram poured out his great worry to the Lord. Sarai, his wife, did not seem to be able to have children. "I have no son. One of my slaves' sons must be my heir."

Gently, God took Abram outside the tent and said, "Look at the sky and try to count the stars; you will have as many descendants as that." Abram trusted God. He knew in his heart that God's plan would be fulfilled. This pleased the Lord, and from that time on Abram's great faith in God made him a just man, accepted by God as a friend.

Genesis 11:31-32; 12; 13; 14; 15: 1-7

Abram Pleads for Lot

ABRAM WAS WORRIED about his nephew Lot. He was an honest man and faithful to God. But he was weak and too often inclined to take the easy way out. He was still living in the city of Sodom and things were getting worse down there in the Jordan Valley. It was known far and wide that the people of Sodom seemed incapable of even the simplest act of kindness and honesty. They led corrupt and wicked lives and were not prepared to let anyone stand in the way of their pleasures. Yet Lot lived in the city and was trying to live a normal family life.

Then the Lord made himself known again to Abram and said that he was going to destroy the wicked cities of Sodom and Gomorrah. Abram immediately thought of his nephew Lot. "Are you really going to destroy the innocent people as well as the guilty?" Abram asked. In pity God heard Abram's cry. So before destroying the cities he sent two of his angels, looking like men, to see if there were any good men still living there. He would spare all the others if there were only ten men worth saving.

Lot was sitting at the city gate when the messengers from God arrived. Immediately he sensed that there was something special about them. He jumped to his feet. "Please stay at my house tonight. In the morning you can get up early and go on your way."

The men declined his offer. "It's kind of you, but we'll sleep in the city square." But Lot was worried about what might happen to them in the dangerous city and urged them to stay with him. They agreed and Lot's servants prepared a splendid meal for them.

But their arrival had not gone unnoticed. Word went around that there were strangers in the city. The men of Sodom had an evil and brutal idea of fun. Here was a chance to enjoy some violent and wicked sport. A mob of chanting men gathered outside Lot's house and battered on the door demanding that the strangers be brought out.

Lot was terrified. "These men are my guests," he shouted back. He knew he must protect his guests. He then stepped outside the door and tried to pacify the seething, dangerous crowd.

The crowd would not listen. They surged forward and those at the front tried to knock Lot out of the way and break the door down. In the nick of time Lot's guests quickly opened the door and pulled Lot inside and slammed it shut again. Then, using powers given them by God, they struck the mob with a form of blindness. They were in uproar, but they could no longer find the door.

"Quick," said the messengers from God. "Take your wife, daughters and any other relatives living in the city and get them out of here! The Lord has sent us to destroy this place completely. Head for the hills so that you are out of danger! Whatever you do, don't look back."

But Lot was afraid. "Please, not the hills!" he begged. "You have saved my life, but I could never make it that far! The disaster will overtake us before we get there. You see that little town over there? I could make it that far. We'll be safe there."

The angel answered, "Very well. We will not destroy that town, but hurry."

The sun was rising when they reached the little town of Zoar. Suddenly the skies seemed to break with a great crack. There was a thunderous roar as the ground around Sodom and Gomorrah opened up in a terrible gaping earthquake. Burning sulphur rained down from the sky, consuming everything in its path.

Lot's wife, ignoring the angel's warning, looked back to see the valley in flames. That was the last she ever saw. She died where she stood looking down over the devastated valley, turned, it is said, into a pillar of rock salt.

Genesis 18: 16-33; 19: 1-29

The Lost Cities
Sodom and Gomorrah, together with Admah, Zeboiim and Zoar, were called the cities of the plain because they grew up in the fertile valley-country watered by the River Jordan. Archaeologists now believe that they lie buried under the shallow water of the southern tip of the Dead Sea.

In about the year 2000 BC there appears to have been a catastrophe which completely emptied the area for at least six hundred years. This was probably a violent earthquake and explosion of gases, followed by a rain of rock salt, ash and dust from the blast.

Then the Lord rained on Sodom and Gomorrah brimstone and fire from the Lord out of heaven; and he overthrew those cities, and all the valley, and all the inhabitants of the cities, and what grew on the ground. Genesis 19:24

Hagar and Ishmael

ABRAM AND SARAI HAD NO CHILDREN. It was becoming difficult to understand how Abram was going to be the father of a great nation while Sarai herself felt abandoned by God. Finally, almost out of desperation, she decided they must do what many other people did in those days. She had an Egyptian maid called Hagar. Abram must take Hagar as a sort of second wife so that she could have a child by him. Because Hagar was Sarai's maid, the child would be considered hers.

Abram agreed. When Hagar knew she was going to have a baby, she became contemptuous of the childless Sarai and sneered at her mistress.

Sarai was upset. She turned on Abram. "It's your fault Hagar looks down on me. Ever since she knew she was going to have a baby she has despised me, even though I gave her to you in the first place."

Abram knew the law of the times. It said that his wife could have Hagar back as her servant. So, fearing more trouble, he let his wife take control of the slave. But Sarai took advantage of her position of power and treated Hagar very badly. Before long things got so bad that Hagar could bear it no longer. She fled southwards to the desert where she might make her way back to Egypt.

While Hagar was resting by a spring in an oasis, an angel appeared to her. "Where have you come from and where are you going?" the angel asked. "I'm running away from my mistress," Hagar replied. "Go back to Sarai your mistress, Hagar," the angel told her. "You will have a son and through him I will give you more descendants than anyone can count. God has heard your cries of distress, and you will call your baby son Ishmael which means 'God hears'." Hagar was amazed. "I have had a vision of God," she said, "and I am still alive!" She returned to the camp

and sure enough, when her time came, Hagar gave birth to a baby boy. Abram was proud of his son.

It was not until some years later that Sarai was able to have a child, just as God had promised. Abram and Sarai were overjoyed to have a child of their own. They called him Isaac.

Sarai still harboured bad feelings towards her servant and did not like the idea of the two children growing up together. More than that, she hated the idea that young Ishmael would inherit some of Abram's wealth. The legal way round the problem would be for Ishmael to take his freedom rather than the inheritance. Sarai decided she would make them go free whether they wanted to or not. She spoke to Abram. "Send the slave girl and her son away. I don't want Ishmael to get any of your money. It must all go to Isaac." Abram was very unhappy. Ishmael was also his son and he loved him.

But God comforted Abram. "Do not be worried about Ishmael and Hagar. Do whatever Sarai says, because it is Isaac who will carry on your line. I also plan to give many, many children to this son of the servant girl. His descendants will become a nation too."

So Abram sent the distressed Hagar and her son off into the desert with food and water. They wandered aimlessly around in the blistering heat until their water gave out. They could not survive for long. Soon Ishmael collapsed and Hagar laid him down under a bush out of the sun. She moved away where she could not see him, "I cannot watch the child die," she cried.

Suddenly a voice spoke to her. "Don't worry Hagar," it said, "God has heard your boy crying. Go and get him and comfort him. He is going to live because God has said 'I will make a great nation from Ishmael'."

As God's messenger finished speaking, Hagar saw that there was a well nearby. Their lives were saved. She put some water in her leather bottle and gave it to Ishmael, who soon recovered.

Although Hagar and Ishmael survived, they never returned to Abram and Sarai. They travelled as far as the Desert of Paran where Ishmael grew up. He became a skilful hunter. As time passed he married an Egyptian girl and started a family. In time his family became a powerful tribe—the Ishmaelites.
Genesis 16 : 1-12 ; 21 : 8-21

When the water in the skin was gone, she cast the child under one of the bushes. Then she went, and sat down over against him a good way off . . . for she said: "Let me not look upon the death of the child."
Genesis 21 : 15

A Son for Abraham

THE STORY OF ISAAC BEGINS in the middle of the story of Hagar and Ishmael. Ishmael was a lively boy and Abram was beginning to think that the lad would become his sole heir, and eventually take over leadership of the tribe. After all, Abram was already very old and his wife was well past normal child-bearing age.

Then the Lord God appeared to him. "Abram," he said, "I am going to make this solemn promise to you. You will be the ancestor of many nations. Because of this I am going to alter your name. From now on you will be called Abraham (which means father of many nations). I will be your God and the God of your children. This land in which you are now a foreigner will belong to your descendants for ever and I will be their God.

"As a special sign of this promise between us I want all your descendants to carry a mark. When they are eight days old every male, including slaves, must be circumcised."

Then the Lord told Abraham: "Your wife also shall have a new name—Sarah. I will make her life overflow with joy because she is going to have a son. She will be the mother of a great nation. There will even be kings among her descendants!"

Abraham was astounded. He bowed his head before the Lord, but as he thought about his old wife having a baby—he couldn't help it—he started laughing! It was ridiculous he told himself. He asked God: "Why not let Ishmael be my heir?" But God replied: "No! Your wife Sarah will have a baby boy this time next year. Call him Isaac. It is his family that will inherit my promise. But I will look after Ishmael. His own descendants will become another great nation."

About three months later God confirmed this promise to Abraham in an even more remarkable way. Abraham was resting at the door of his tent in the hottest part of the day. He looked up and saw three men standing under the trees near the camp. With Eastern hospitality Abraham ran over to them, and bowing low said, "Please don't pass without stopping to wash your feet and eat a meal with us." The men accepted with thanks.

A meal was hastily prepared and Abraham himself served them. While the four of them ate, one of the visitors said suddenly, "Where is your wife Sarah?" "In the tent," replied Abraham. "Nine months from now," went on the man "I will return and Sarah, your wife, will have a son." Abraham suddenly realized these men were no ordinary visitors.

Inside the tent, Sarah heard what the man said. She chuckled to herself. "Me have a baby at my age! I am far too old."

But the man knew what Sarah was thinking and asked Abraham, "Why does Sarah laugh and think she is too old to have a baby? Is anything too hard for the Lord?" Then both husband and wife knew who was speaking. Frightened, Sarah appeared from the tent and said quickly "No, no. I didn't laugh." "Yes you did Sarah," replied the man. "I heard your thoughts."

As Sarah said happily nine months later when it all came true, Isaac was a good name for their son. It meant laughter. "God has brought me laughter," she smiled. "Everyone who hears about Abraham and me—two old-timers having a baby—will laugh with us!"

When Isaac was eight days old he was circumcised. He grew into a fit, strong boy and Abraham

Then Abraham put forth his hand, and took the knife to slay his son. But the angel of the Lord called to him from heaven, and said, "Abraham, Abraham!" And he said, "Here am I." He said, "Do not lay your hand on the lad or do anything to him; for now I know that you fear God, seeing you have not withheld your son, your only son, from me." And Abraham lifted up his eyes and looked, and behold, behind him was a ram, caught in a thicket by his horns.
Genesis 22: 10–13

loved him dearly. He would have gone to any lengths to make sure he came to no harm. It was a happy ending to Abraham's faith in God.

Abraham is tested again

Now Abraham's faith was put to the test once again. Abraham heard the voice of God saying, "Abraham, I know you love Isaac very much, but I want you to take him with you to the mountains of Moriah and to sacrifice him in my honour."

Abraham was devastated. It seemed that God had given him something, only to take it away again. But he was also convinced that whatever God did or said had a good reason behind it. He must trust his Maker. So he loaded his donkey, called two of his men to go with them, told Isaac to get ready and set off.

On the third day of the journey they came in sight of a high mountain, a fitting place for a sacrifice. "Stay here with the donkey," he said to his servant. Abraham and Isaac collected together the wood they had brought for the sacrifice, the smouldering wood to start the fire and a large sharp knife.

In silence, Abraham and Isaac climbed the mountain. He was sure that he was going to have

to kill his son. Isaac, as yet, had no idea of the turmoil in his father's mind.

"Father, we've got the wood, the fire and everything else, but where's the lamb?" Isaac asked. In anguish, Abraham looked at him. "God has got a sacrifice ready for us," he said grimly. Over and over he said to himself, "God gave us Isaac so that he would be the beginning of a new nation. He promised it. Perhaps Isaac will come back to life again." This faith kept him going.

When they reached the summit, they built an altar of stones. Abraham put the wood on top. Then he took a surprised and bewildered Isaac and laid him on the altar. Still thinking of God's promise, and with a look of great tenderness towards his son, Abraham drew the knife. He was prepared to start the downward swing, when a powerful voice cried out, "Abraham! Abraham!" It was the angel of the Lord.

"Do not lay a hand on the boy! Now I know that you love and obey the Lord your God. You did not refuse him your only son."

Abraham almost collapsed with relief. He took Isaac off the altar and embraced him. Just a short distance away, he saw there was a ram, trapped in the thorns by its horns. God had provided a sacrifice after all.

Rejoicing they returned home, knowing that God did not ask for human sacrifice.
Genesis 18 : 1-15 ; 21 : 1-7 ; 22 : 1-14

The Ceremony of Circumcision
Circumcision is a minor operation to cut away the loose skin covering the end of the penis. It was widely practised by primitive peoples, usually as a sign that a boy had reached manhood. God took this custom and gave it to Abraham as a reminder of their special relationship for all time—every child in Israel was one of God's own people. The ceremony was performed on the eighth day after birth, when the child was also named.

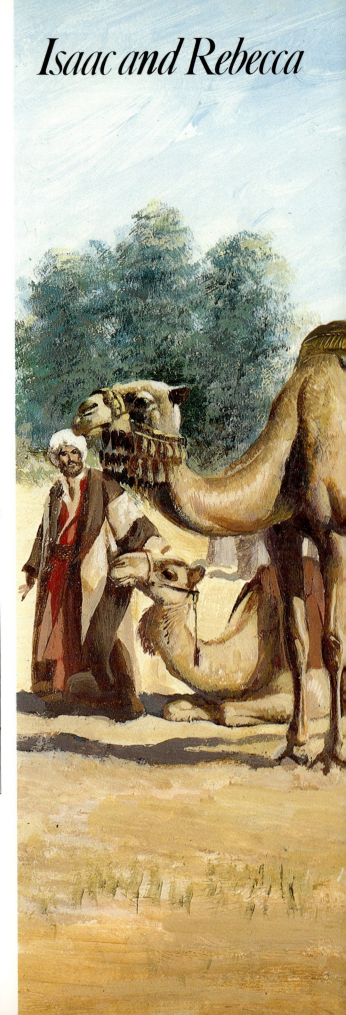

Isaac and Rebecca

SARAH DIED. Abraham bought a piece of land from the Hittite tribe and buried her at Hebron in Canaan. Abraham, too, was a very old man and it was time to find a wife for Isaac. Abraham insisted that Isaac should marry someone from among his relatives back in his home country. It was important that Isaac should worship God as his father had done. If he married a local Canaanite girl, she would bring pagan ways into the family. So Abraham summoned his most faithful servant and told him to go and find a suitable bride from among Abraham's family in Mesopotamia.

Abraham was confident that God would guide him to the right person.

The servant set off with a caravan of camels laden with presents of rich clothes and jewellery. When he arrived in the part of the country where Abraham's brother had lived, he stopped at a well outside one of the cities. There he made the camels kneel and waited. It was late afternoon and soon all the town's young girls would come to the well to fetch water.

Abraham's servant breathed a prayer to his master's God. "Lord God, please give me success today in my mission and keep your promise to my

master Abraham. I will ask one of the young women who come for water, to give me a drink. If she also offers to draw water for my camels, may she be the girl you have chosen for Isaac."

As soon as he had finished praying a beautiful young girl came out to the well. She went to the well and filled the water jar. Abraham's servant went up to her and said, "Please, can I have a drink from your jar?"

"Drink, Sir," she replied, lowering the heavy earthenware jar. When he finished she said, "I'll fill up the jar again and give some water to your camels too, if you like." She poured the rest of the water into the animals' trough, refilled the jar, and filled it again and again until the camels had had enough. As he watched, Abraham's servant knew that this was the girl he had come to find.

When she had finished, the man brought out a fine, gold nose-ring and two heavy bracelets. He gave them to the astonished girl and said, "Please tell me who your father is and if he will give me shelter for the night." "My father is Bethuel, son of Nahor," she answered. The servant was overjoyed—Nahor was Abraham's own brother.

Rebecca ran home and told everyone the news that a servant of Abraham had arrived. Her brother, Laban, saw the rings and bracelets and ran to the well to invite the servant to stay.

That evening, the family gathered for a great meal. But the servant said to Laban and his father: "I will not eat until I have said what I have to say." He told them all about Abraham and Sarah and the way God had blessed and protected them. He described how Abraham had told him to find a wife for Isaac from his own people and also how he had met Rebecca.

Bethuel and Laban were sure that God had led the man to their house. "Since the Lord has sent you, what can we say? Here is Rebecca. Take her and go. We are happy for her to marry your master's son, just as God has planned."

When the servant heard this, he praised God for the way things had turned out. Then he unpacked beautiful gifts—fine robes, silver, gold and jewels—and gave them to Rebecca. He gave gifts to her brother and mother too.

Next morning they prepared to leave. But Laban and his mother did not want to lose Rebecca so soon. "Let Rebecca stay here for a week or so and then she can go," they said. But the servant was eager to get home after his successful mission. So they asked Rebecca what she wanted to do. She said she was ready to go there and then.

So the group of travellers prepared for the journey back to Canaan.

Some days later, back in Canaan, Isaac was walking in the fields, when he saw a camel train approaching. He recognized it as his father's.

Rebecca, looking into the distance and eager for her first glimpse of her new home, saw the young man. "Who is that man coming to us across the fields?" she asked. "He is my master's son," replied the servant. There in the fields surrounding the family encampment, the couple met for the first time. Rebecca's beauty won Isaac's heart at once.

Before long they were married. It was more than just an arranged marriage. They knew that they loved each other deeply.
Genesis 24

Then his father Isaac said to him, "Come near and kiss me, my son." So he came near and kissed him; and he smelled the smell of his garments, and blessed him.
Genesis 27:26

Esau and Jacob

REBECCA GAVE BIRTH TO TWO FINE BOYS, twins, who were very different from each other. Esau was older than Jacob by just a few minutes. He grew up to be a sturdy outdoor boy, fond of hunting. He was dark-skinned and hairy. Jacob was smooth-skinned. He was quiet and studious and stayed in the company of his mother. Esau was Isaac's favourite, while Rebecca preferred Jacob.

About this time Abraham died at a ripe old age. Isaac and Ishmael met again at his burial service on the land where Abraham himself had buried Sarah. All Abraham's wealth was passed to Isaac. Now Esau, as the eldest son (even though only by a few minutes) owned the birthright. This meant that he would inherit all the family possessions and privileges when Isaac died. He couldn't care less about this. But Jacob would have given almost anything for the rights to the family leadership.

Then, suddenly, one day, an opportunity presented itself. It was evening and Jacob was cooking a tasty bean soup. Esau burst into the tent hot and hungry after a day's hunting. The smell of the cooking almost drove him wild. "Quick!" he gasped, "Give me some of that red stuff. I'm famished." Jacob looked at him steadily and made no effort to ladle out the food. "I'll do a deal with you," he said. "I'll give you the food, if you give me your rights as first born son."

"All right," Esau said hurriedly. "I'll starve if I don't eat and a lot of use my rights will be then. Come on, give me something to eat."

But Jacob was not going to be hurried. "You have to swear that you will let me be counted as the first born." Esau could not be bothered with this nonsense and so he humoured his twin brother. "I swear," he said. He snatched the bowl of soup and ate ravenously. Then he drank some wine and left the tent, the whole episode quite forgotten.

In fact no more mention was made of Esau's promise and Jacob's trickery until Isaac grew old. As the old man became weaker his sight dwindled until he became blind. Of course he had no idea of what had gone on between his sons. But Rebecca knew.

One day Isaac called Esau to him. "Son," he said, "I've not got long to live. Take your bow and arrows and go and kill some fresh meat for my supper. Cook it the way I like and then I will give you the special blessing that will make you head of the family." Off went Esau; he didn't need to be asked twice. Rebecca, who had been listening, smiled. Here was a chance to make sure *her* favourite became head of the family.

Hurriedly she told Jacob to kill two kids from the flock. "I'll make the tasty dish your father likes." Then she explained how Jacob would pretend to be Esau, so that the blind Isaac would give *him* his blessing. "But father will touch me," said Jacob. "Then he will be sure to know I'm not Esau." But Rebecca had an answer to that too. She dressed him in Esau's clothes and put some rough goat skins on his arms and shoulders so that, to a blind man, he would seem hairy. Then she handed Jacob the stew and pushed him into the tent.

"Father," he said in greeting. "Which of you is it?" old Isaac asked. "It's Esau," he lied. "Here is the food you asked for. I've come to give it to you and receive your blessing." Isaac was a bit puzzled. The voice did not seem quite right. "Come closer so I can touch you." He was reassured. This did seem like his rough, hairy son Esau. "You are sure you're Esau? Your voice sounds like Jacob's." "I'm Esau," Jacob said.

So Isaac took the food and afterwards he pronounced the solemn blessing on his son. It gave his son leadership of the family and control of all the family riches and herds. It was as legally binding as if it had been said in a court room.

The plan had worked. Jacob left the tent, just as Esau arrived fresh from the hunt. Esau took the animal he had caught and cooked a wonderful meal for his father, anxious now for his blessing. "Please father, sit up and eat the food I've brought. Then you can give me a blessing," he said entering the tent. "Who are you?" Isaac demanded of the astonished young man. "I'm Esau, your first born son," he said. Isaac began to tremble. "Then who was it who just came in and gained my blessing?"

Esau guessed at once. His brother had tricked him out of the family rights and fortune! "Father, give me your blessing too!" he shouted desperately.

"I can't," his father said. "I've already given it to Jacob. There's nothing I can do about it." "Haven't you got anything for me at all?" "No," Isaac replied. "I've already made Jacob master over you; there is nothing I can do."

Esau went away in a fury. He had nothing but hate in his heart for his cunning brother. As soon as their father was dead, he would be revenged. But he planned without the scheming of his mother Rebecca. *Genesis 25: 24-34; 27: 1-41*

Jacob Leaves Home

JACOB WAS IN TROUBLE. Esau, his brother, was planning his revenge for cheating him of his birthright. "You'd better flee and stay with my brother Laban in Haran until Esau's rage has cooled down," his mother said. Jacob agreed readily. Rebecca then put the suggestion to her husband Isaac. "Jacob needs a wife," she said. "But we cannot have him marrying one of these Canaanite women as Esau has." Isaac agreed. He wanted his sons to worship God like their grandfather Abraham. So he sent for Jacob and told him to travel to Mesopotamia to his uncle Laban and to find a wife there.

Stairway to heaven

Jacob set off. It was a long journey, but because of his fear of Esau he travelled as far as he could the first day. That night he pitched camp and lay down to sleep. But his sleep was not peaceful—he had the strangest dream. He dreamt he saw a stairway, just like that on the great temples of those days. Enormously high, it reached up into the heavens. The stairway was crowded with angels going up towards heaven, or coming down to earth. The Lord God stood above it. "I am the Lord, the God of Abraham and Isaac," God said. "I will give the land you are lying on to you and to your descendants. They will be as many as there are specks of dust on the earth." The Lord promised to be with Jacob, protecting him wherever he went.

This experience changed Jacob's life. "God is in this very place," he said "and I did not know it." Early the next morning Jacob took the stone he had been lying on and set it up as a memorial. He called the place Bethel, 'the house of God'. Then he made God a solemn promise. "If you protect me and bring me back safely to my father's house, you will be my God. I will worship you and give you a tenth of all that I have."

Continuing on his journey, Jacob came in sight of his destination. There stood a well with a group of shepherds standing round it, waiting to roll back the large stone covering the entrance. Jacob came up and greeted the shepherds, and asked them if they knew his uncle Laban. "Yes we do," they replied, "and here comes his daughter Rachel with his flocks now."

As she drew near, Jacob approached Rachel. She was the most beautiful girl he had ever seen. "They tell me you are Rachel, daughter of Laban. I will water your flock for you." Jacob rolled the great stone from the mouth of the well so that water could be drawn for the sheep to drink. Then with a cry of laughter, he gave Rachel a greeting kiss and said. "I am Jacob the son of Rebecca, your father's sister. Tell Laban I am here."

Rachel ran to tell her father and Laban rushed out to meet his nephew. Jacob was immediately invited home. He stayed with the family for a month. Before long, Jacob had fallen in love with the beautiful Rachel.

Laban was very friendly towards Jacob and it was soon decided that Jacob should stay and work for him. "What wages shall I give you?" he asked Jacob. "I will work seven years without payment," replied Jacob, " if I can then marry your daughter Rachel." Laban agreed happily and Jacob set off into the pasture land to look after the flocks.

Jacob was so much in love with Rachel that the seven years flew by. When the time was up he went to Laban to arrange the marriage.

The day for the marriage was set. There was to be a ceremony followed by feasting and dancing. All the family would be there, together with neighbours and servants.

But Laban had decided to trick Jacob. Rachel had an elder sister called Leah. She was not nearly so beautiful as Rachel. When the feasting was over, Jacob retired to his tent to wait for his bride. Soon there was a rustle in the darkness and he heard her enter.

In the morning Jacob looked over to his new wife sleeping softly beside him. He got a terrible shock. It was not Rachel, but Leah!

In a fury Jacob rushed out to find Laban. "What do you think you are doing? I have worked for you seven years to marry Rachel. You agreed to that and now you've given me Leah!

Jacob loved Rachel; and he said, "I will
serve you seven years for your younger
daughter Rachel." Laban said, "It is better
that I give her to you than that I should
give her to any other man; stay with me."
So Jacob served seven years for Rachel, and
they seemed to him but a few days, because
of the love he had for her.
Genesis 29:18–20

Why have you tricked me?"

Laban tried to calm Jacob. "Jacob," he said, "there's a custom in these parts that says the elder daughter must always get married before her younger sister." Jacob the schemer had been outwitted. There was nothing he could do but to accept the situation.

"I'll make another deal with you," said Laban. "Wait for the week of the marriage celebrations to end and then you may marry Rachel too—on one condition. You must work for me for another seven years."

Seven years! But Jacob accepted for he still wanted Rachel for his wife. And so they were married. Jacob and Rachel were happy to belong to each other at last. But Leah was unhappy. She was pushed into second place by her sister.

The Lord took pity on Leah for, within a few years, she and Jacob had four sons. She was delighted and praised God because he had been so good to her.

Rachel became jealous. "I want children, Jacob," she shouted at him angrily. "Do you expect me to play God?" Jacob replied. "He is the one who gives life or withholds it."

So Rachel said, "Take my slave girl Bilhah as your wife. She can have children for me." Jacob did so and Bilhah bore him two sons. Rachel was overjoyed.

Leah now gave Jacob her own slave girl Zilpah who gave Jacob two sons as well. Now there were eight sons. But the rivalry between the sisters continued. Leah had another son, her fifth, and then a daughter, and yet another son. It was then that God answered Rachel's prayers and she gave birth to Jacob's eleventh son. They named him Joseph. Of all his sons, Joseph was Jacob's favourite.

Soon after Joseph's birth the call of Jacob's home in the south became strong. Jacob faced Laban. "I've worked hard for you all these years and built up your flocks so that you are a rich man," he said. "I've earned my wives and children. Let me take them and go home."

Laban pretended to be grateful for all the work Jacob had done. He insisted on paying him a wage for his work. But Jacob said, "I do not want payment. Just let me have all the black lambs and all the spotted or streaky coloured goats. That will be enough for me. And I will work for you a little while longer."

"Agreed," said Laban. "Let's do that." But even while he was arranging the deal with Jacob,

---

Marriage Customs

A code of law drawn up by King Hammurabi of Babylon in about 1700 BC contains a number of rules concerning marriage. It is clear from the Bible that Abraham also observed these rules which state:

● A man must not take a second wife unless the first wife is unable to have children.

● The husband may take a secondary wife (a concubine), or his wife may give him a slave-girl to have children by her.

● The children of the slave-girl may not be sent away.

In Jacob and Esau's time people were allowed more than one wife.

Marriage was a civil rather than a religious affair. When a couple became engaged a contract was made before two witnesses. Sometimes the couple gave one another a ring or bracelet. A sum of money, a bride-price, had to be paid to the girl's father. It could sometimes be paid partly in work by the man. The girl's father, in return, gave her or her husband a dowry. This could be servants, land or property.

The custom of marrying off the eldest daughter before her younger sisters is not known outside this story. It may well have been another of Laban's tricks on Jacob.

Laban was planning to steal from him. He instructed his sons to take all the black lambs and coloured goats out of the herd and drive them miles away. When Jacob came to inspect the animals that were to be his there were none left. He would now have to wait for new young to be born to see how many black, spotted or streaky animals there were.

By clever breeding, Jacob again built up a large flock of coloured goats and lambs. And he saw to it that they were the strongest animals. Soon Jacob became very rich and bought camels and asses and servants. But Laban's sons thought that Jacob had got rich through trickery and complained. Jacob answered: "Your father deceived me over Leah and Rachel. If I have succeeded it is with God's help. Now the Lord orders me to return to Canaan."

Jacob did not tell Laban that he was going to return home. Early one morning, while Laban was away shearing his sheep, Jacob gathered all his herdsmen together and with his camels, donkeys, sheep and goats he and his family set off for Canaan. He took only what belonged to him. He did not know that Rachel had hidden Laban's household idols in her saddlebag.

It was three days before Laban heard the news of his wily son-in-law's departure. He acted quickly. He was not going to let Jacob get away. He set off with his men in pursuit but it was seven days before they caught up with Jacob.

Laban shouted at Jacob, "Why did you deceive me and take my daughters without so much as a goodbye? And why have you stolen my family idols?" Jacob was angry. Not knowing that Rachel had taken the idols, he vowed he would kill anyone found with Laban's property.

Laban searched the camp but could find nothing. He even searched Rachel's tent. She pretended she was not well, but she was sitting on a saddle-bag in which she had hidden the gods. By this time Jacob had grown really angry.

"What right have you to hunt me down?" he stormed. "What have I done to you? I've worked all these years for your daughters and for your flocks. I have been outside night and day in all weathers. Any losses the flocks have suffered I repaid out of my own pocket. Even then you tricked and cheated me. If God was not looking after me, you would have turned me away empty-handed long ago. But God is with me and he will not let you touch me!"

The furious quarrel might have ended in disaster. But both men saw sense and made a pact. They set up a great pile of stones as a boundary, agreeing that neither would ever cross it to attack the other. They agreed that the Lord God would be the judge of their agreement. They sacrificed a goat to God and then sat down to eat a ceremonial meal together.

The next morning Laban kissed his daughters and grandchildren goodbye and returned home. At last Jacob—with God's help—was a free man, and now quite a rich one too. He set off for Canaan and home.
Genesis 27 : 42-46 ; 28 ; 29 ; 30 ; 31

Jacob's Return

AS SOON AS LABAN HAD LEFT, Jacob's camp was thrown into a fever of activity, packing cooking utensils, tents and foodstuffs for the rest of the journey. Now Jacob was in a hurry to be back in Canaan.

One evening, as they travelled, looking for a suitable place to camp, they were again met by angels who looked like men. They assured Jacob that God was still looking after him. Jacob pitched camp there and named it 'God's camp'.

It was at this camp that Jacob decided he must make peace with his brother Esau. God had told him to return to Canaan and his relatives and it was inevitable that the brothers would meet again. Jacob had vivid memories of Esau vowing to kill him because of his trickery.

By now Esau had become a powerful tribal leader. His warriors were tough and Jacob's men, weary from the long journey, would be no match for them should a fight break out. Jacob had no idea what Esau's reactions would be after all this time but he had no reason to believe he would be friendly.

Jacob had to make sure. He despatched messengers to Esau, who was living in Edom. "When you see Esau, say 'I, Jacob, your obedient servant, report to my master Esau, that I have been with Laban all this time but now I wish to come home. I am not poor, I own cattle, sheep, goats and slaves, so I am not looking for favours. I am sending word to ask for your friendship.'"

Some while later the messengers returned. "We met Esau and he is already on his way to meet you. He has a force of 400 men!" The news confirmed Jacob's worst fears.

At once Jacob began to make plans. He divided his herds and his company into two groups so that, should Esau attack one group, the other might be able to escape. He then prayed to God. "Oh Lord, I am on my way home at your command. You promised to look after me and protect me. I know I am not worth all the goodness you have shown me. I left Canaan with nothing and now I have a family, men at my command and large herds of animals—all because you gave them to me. Please save me, I pray. I am afraid that Esau will kill me and my wives and children too. Please remember your promises to me."

The next day Jacob decided to send a present to Esau. From his herds he selected 580 animals and divided them up into four or five small herds. He sent them ahead, instructing his men: "When you see my brother and he asks you where you are going and who the animals belong to, tell him they are a present for him and that I am coming up behind."

Jacob now sent his wives and all the rest of the party ahead to ford the river Jabbok. He himself lingered behind.

That night a strange thing happened. As he tried to sleep, it seemed to him that a stranger, a man, suddenly appeared and picked a fight with him. Soon the two were on the ground both trying to gain the upper hand. They tussled and rolled in the dust. The two seemed evenly matched. As they fought minutes, then hours

And Jacob was left alone; and a man wrestled with him until the breaking of the day. When the man saw that he did not prevail against Jacob, he touched the hollow of his thigh; and Jacob's thigh was put out of joint as he wrestled with him.
Genesis 32 : 24–25

passed by, and still neither could gain the upper hand. Near exhaustion they fought on, under the stars, until daybreak approached.

Slowly, Jacob began to realize that this was no ordinary man. There was something strange—even supernatural—about him. He knew, too, that he must carry on fighting. He must win.

Suddenly, as the sky grew lighter, the man freed one hand and jabbed a short, sharp punch at Jacob's hip. It struck home. With a cry of pain Jacob collapsed to the ground and lay there, his hip dislocated. But still, gritting his teeth through the pain, Jacob held on grimly—determined not to let the man go.

"Let me go!" cried the stranger. But Jacob knew that this man was sent from God and he gasped, "No. Not unless you give me a blessing."

"What is your name?" asked the man. "Jacob," he answered. The stranger replied, "You will no longer be called Jacob. You have struggled with God and with men and you have won. From now on you will be called Israel."

Jacob wanted to know more. "What is your name?" he asked. "Why do you want to know my name?" the man replied. Then he gave Jacob a blessing.

As the man blessed him, it all became clear to Jacob. This was God's blessing! He had so often wrestled with God in his mind—asking for protection and seeking God's guidance. The fight was a sign that he must keep wrestling with God for the answers to his questions. The scheming Jacob must go. As the sun rose, he praised God, in wonder at what had happened.

Jacob rejoined his family. News arrived that Esau and his men had been sighted. Jacob was still afraid.

As Esau approached, Jacob knelt down on the ground and bowed seven times—a greeting, usually reserved for kings. There was a long moment as Esau stood, looking at Jacob. Then, with a shout, he ran forward and threw his arms round his long-lost brother. Completely overcome by emotion, tears coursed down the faces of both men.

Then Esau saw the women and children approaching. "Whose are these?" he asked. "These are the children God has been good enough to give me," Jacob answered. He beckoned them forward and they came, one by one, to meet their uncle.

"And what did you mean by all those cattle you sent on ahead?" asked Esau. "They are for you, to show you that I want to be friends again," Jacob answered.

"Oh Jacob, you keep them. I have enough." Esau told him.

"No please, you take them. It means so much to me that you have forgiven me." As Jacob insisted, Esau accepted the gifts.

So, having met and talked of all that had happened since their youth, the time came for the brothers to part. Esau tried to persuade Jacob to follow him home. But Jacob could not move so quickly with children and young animals. He agreed to follow on later. Then, hugging each other once more they said their good-byes.

Eventually Jacob, his family and his herds arrived in the land of Canaan, settling in the centre at a place called Shechem. There he bought land and set up an altar to worship God. And now he could call the Lord God, not only the God of his fathers Abraham and Isaac but the God of Israel too.

Genesis 32; 33

Jacob's new name

Israel comes from the Hebrew name *yisra'el* and means 'God struggles'. God's comment was "Your name will no longer be Jacob. You have struggled with God and with men and you have won; so your name will be Israel." (*Genesis 32:28*).

A man's name was extremely important, as it related to his personality and to his fortune in life. Only a superior could change a person's name and then only to record a profound change in the person or his circumstances. So, Jacob's change of name became the moment when Jacob the trickster becomes Israel, the father of God's people.

*Esau ran to meet him, and embraced him,
and fell on his neck and kissed him, and they
wept.*
Genesis 33 : 4

Jacob's Sons

WHILE JACOB AND HIS FAMILY were travelling on to Canaan, Rachel gave birth to a second son. "Call him Benoni, 'child of my sorrow,'" she said, as she knew that she was dying. Jacob buried his beloved wife and called his son Benjamin, "son of my right hand".

Benjamin and Joseph, his other son by Rachel, were Jacob's favourites. This made the other children jealous.

At the age of seventeen Joseph helped his brothers look after the sheep and goats. They had no time for him. In fact they hated him.

Joseph was a sneak. If the brothers were slack in their work with the herds, it got back to Jacob because Joseph told him. And to make matters worse Jacob had given his son a magnificent coat decorated in bright colours—a rare thing in the desert region. Every time they saw it, the brothers hated Joseph more.

Things came to a head one morning when Joseph told his brothers about a vivid dream he had had. "I dreamt that all twelve of us were in the harvest field binding wheat sheaves and laying them on the ground. Mine stood up and your sheaves formed a circle and bowed down to it."

His brothers couldn't take this. "Who do you think you are?" they shouted at him. "Are you going to be a great king and rule over us?" Their hatred of him deepened.

Then Jacob had another dream in which the sun, the moon and eleven stars all bowed down to him. He told everyone in the family about it. His father was shocked. "Do you mean that one day your mother, brothers and I will bow down to you?" Jacob was saddened by his son's arrogance and the brothers could not wait to get their own back on him.

Before long, their chance came. They were out on the plain with the herds when Jacob sent Joseph out to see how they were doing. They saw his wonderful multi-coloured coat a long way off and it gave them time to hatch a plot. "Here comes the dreamer!" they jeered. "Let's kill him. If we throw his body down one of these dry wells we can pretend a wild animal killed him. Then we'll see what happens to his dreams!"

But Reuben, the eldest, pleaded for Joseph's life. "No, don't let's kill him. Throw him down a well but don't hurt him." Reuben planned to come back later and rescue him. The others agreed and Reuben left to look after the herds.

As Joseph came up, his brothers seized him, ripped off his coat and threw him down a well. Then they sat down to eat. On the horizon they could see a caravan of traders approaching. As the riders drew near, one of the brothers had an idea.

"We won't gain anything by killing our brother," he said. "Why don't we sell him to these traders as a slave?" Everyone agreed, so they hauled Joseph out of the well, hailed the caravan's leader and sold Joseph for twenty pieces of silver. The traders were on their way to Egypt where they knew they could get a good price for a healthy young man like Joseph.

As the traders rode off with their prize Reuben returned. He went to the well but it was empty. Quickly he found his brothers who told him what had happened. Reuben was relieved that Joseph was at least alive. Together they prepared to fool their father by killing a goat and splashing the blood on Joseph's coat.

Arriving home they brought the torn, filthy and bloody garment to old Jacob. "We found this," they said. "Is it Joseph's coat?"

Jacob recognized it immediately. Nothing could console him. He wept and wept, tearing his clothes and covering himself with ashes. But the brothers were not really sorry for what they had done. At last Joseph—the main source of irritation all these years—was out of the way and their father might pay them some attention.

And so, at seventeen, Joseph was on his way to the most prosperous land in the world of those days, the country of great kings and huge pyramids—Egypt. It may have seemed a disaster to the young man, but God had a reason for sending him there and many adventures were in store for him. It was not going to be an easy time, but in the end his dreams would come true. Just as he had said, the whole family would bow to him. And he would be able to save their lives, making sure God's promises to Abraham came true.

Genesis 37

So when Joseph came to his brothers, they stripped him of his robe, the long robe with sleeves that he wore; and they took him and cast him into a pit. The pit was empty, there was no water in it. Then they sat down to eat; and looking up they saw a caravan of Ishmaelites coming from Gilead. . . . Then Judah said to his brothers, "What profit is it if we slay our brother and conceal his blood? Come, let us sell him to the Ishmaelites, and let not our hand be upon him, for he is our brother, our own flesh."
Genesis 37 : 23–27

DATE CHART

BC	MESOPOTAMIA	PALESTINE	EGYPT
6000-4500	NEW STONE AGE (NEOLITHIC)		
	Nineveh: Pottery and houses found.	Jericho, 5000: Cult objects, shrines and brick-built houses.	
4500-3400	'COPPER-STONE' PERIOD (CHALCOLITHIC)		
	Tell Halaf, Carchemish and Tepe Gawra: 1st Sumerian city-states. Ur, Uruk: Trade to India and Asia. Writing on clay. Stone-built temples.	Jericho: Painted pottery and mural painting. Beersheba: copper industry. Large numbers of nomadic tribes.	The Badari: Animals domesticated. Wide trading. Fine jewellers. Amratians cultivate Nile valley. Make copper and ivory objects. Garzeans cast metal tools and weapons. 1st hieroglyphs.
	EARLY BRONZE AGE		
3400-2000 c2371 -2255 2113-2006	Sumerian kings rule in Ur. King Sargon founds Akkadian empire which stretches from Persia to the Mediterranean. 3rd dynasty of Ur. Oldest known law code.	Northern towns develop: Megiddo and Tell el Farah. Forests cleared leaving desert. Civilization destroyed by the Amorites, a nomadic tribe.	Menes unifies Egypt c2900. Memphis is capital. Old Kingdom c2686-2181. Pyramids built. Trade with Lebanon and Media.
2100-1550	MIDDLE BRONZE AGE		
	Ur sacked. 1st dynasty of Babylon. Hammurabi king 1792-1750	Abraham comes to Palestine. Isaac born. Jacob born. Joseph born.	Middle kingdom c2133-1633 Egypt thrives. Hyksos kings 1674-1567
1550-1200	LATE BRONZE AGE		
	Kassite dynasty.	Jacob's family to Egypt.	New kingdom 1567-1085

GLOSSARY

INDEX

ALTAR a place for offering sacrifices to God. Israelite altars were usually simple mounds of earth or a block of stone supported by a pile of smaller stones.

BLESSING to the Hebrew people the father's blessing had a special importance. The blessing Isaac gave his son was a passing on of the promises God had given to Abraham—that from him a great nation would spring. The Hebrews believed that any word that was said with real intention and solemnity could never be withdrawn. It was as definite as any action. So Isaac could not withdraw his blessing from Jacob, cunning cheat though he was.

BOUNDARY line dividing two areas of country, often marked by standing stones or piles of rock.

CARAVAN an armed group of traders and travellers on camels and pack donkeys travelling together usually through the desert. The ancient world was crisscrossed by well marked caravan routes.

CHERUBIM winged angelic creatures often used to guard and protect sacred objects. They are shown in ancient carvings as huge lion-like creatures with human heads and wings.

CREATOR the first 'person' to start or make something. God is called the Creator because he made everything that exists.

DOWRY a gift given to the bride by her father. It remained her possession until her death when it passed to her sons or back to her family if she had none. During her life it was administered by her husband.

FAMINE scarcity of food caused by drought or other disasters.

HEIR the person, usually the eldest son, who is to inherit a man's wealth when he dies.

IDOL an image of a god made of wood, stone or metal. Associated with pagan ceremonies of worship.

MEMORIAL a monument or object erected to remind the community of an important event or person.

NOAH'S SONS the Hebrews believed that the races of the ancient Near East were each descended from one or other of Noah's three sons. Shem was the ancestor of the Semites; from Japeth came Indo-European races. The Hamites settled mainly in Africa, in Egypt and Ethiopia.

NOMAD a people who are permanently travelling, moving their livestock from pasture to pasture.

OASIS a place where water occurs naturally in the desert. Sometimes inhabited, used as a stopping-place for travellers.

PAGAN people who do not believe in God.

PITCH a black resinous substance found naturally in the Middle East. It is liquid when hot, but cools to form a hard waterproof mass. This makes it ideal for caulking ships' hulls.

SACRIFICE something offered to God as an expression of thanks. Sometimes a freshly killed animal is offered on an altar as a sign of repentance.

SATAN traditional name for the prince of evil—the Devil. It means 'adversary' and implies that he is opposed to God.

TEMPLE a building in which to worship God or gods.

UNIVERSE all that God created.

A view of the Dead Sea from the Yehuda Desert. The rift valley of the River Jordan stretches from Lake Galilee in the north to the Dead Sea in the south and continues on to the Gulf of Aqaba. The Dead Sea, known in Old Testament times as the Salt Sea because of its water's heavy deposits of salt, is the lowest point of the earth's surface. Lot settled with his family "in the cities of the plain" in the fertile valley near the Dead Sea. Photo: Zefa

BLACK SEA

• Hattusa

**HITTITE
KINGDOM**

Halys

*Lake
Tuz*

TAURUS MOUNTAINS

Carchemish •

2 • Haran

Orontes

Euphrates

CYPRUS

THE GREAT SEA
(MEDITERRANIAN SEA)

Byblos •

Sidon • **PHOENICIA** • Damascus

Tyre • • Dan

Jordan

Dothan • 5

Shechem • 3 • Penuel

Bethel • Ai

Jerusalem • • Jericho

CANAAN *Dead*

Gaza • Hebron *Sea* 4

• 3

Beer-sheba **MOAB**

EDOM

EGYPT

• On
• Memphis

Pyramids near
Memphis

**SINAI
PENINSULA**

• Ezion-geber

Nile

Moses receiving the
tablets of law on
Mount Sinai

RED SEA

1 Abraham's father
came from Ur. Its
temple tower—a
stairway leading to
heaven—is a re-
minder of the Tower
of Babel.

2 Abraham, obeying
God, left Haran and
travelled to Canaan.

3 Shechem, Bethel,
Hebron and Beer-
sheba were the main
encampments of
Abraham, Isaac and
Jacob.

4 Lot settled at Sodom
by the Dead Sea. The
wicked city was
destroyed.

5 At Dothan Joseph
was sold by his
brother to merchants
travelling to Egypt.

"Go from your country. . ."
In obedience to a command from God, Abraham
and his family left the comforts of civilization to
become nomads. They set out for Canaan which
in time would become the Promised Land.